Hard Corals Jim Fatherree

Introduction

The world's coral reefs are some of the most beautiful and fascinating environments on Earth, and the diversity of life on the reef is rivaled only by that of the tropical rainforest. When we picture the dazzling array of organisms in these microcosms and the complex interactions between them, most of us would never dream that such a wonderful assortment of creatures could be kept alive and healthy in a home aquarium. However, in the last ten years or so improved methods of collection and delivery and improved husbandry techniques and equipment have made this dream possible for even the beginning aquarist. These attempts at reproductions of the complex reef are commonly known as reef or mini-reef aquariums. Well stocked modern reef aquariums typically house a broad assortment of plants and animals belonging to several biological groups including fish, crabs and shrimp, worms, snails and clams, sea anemones, corals and algae. When done right, all of these organisms can do more than just survive in an aquarium; they can thrive and even reproduce.

This book is intended to be a guide that helps you become more familiar with one of the major components of any reef aquarium, the stony corals, also widely known as hard corals. These corals are some of the most impressive and interesting animals available to aquarists, but they can also be some of the most difficult to care for. Many corals simply are very delicate, while some others can kill anything they touch. Some need very intense lighting, others don't. There's a lot of very important information to learn about each kind! For this reason in the following sections we will cover the biology of these animals, the basic equipment and materials needed to care for them and how to choose "good" specimens to add to your own reef.

© by T.F.H. Publications, Inc.

Distributed in the UNITED STATES to the Pet Trade by T.F.H. Publications, Inc., One T.F.H. Plaza, Neptune City, NJ 07753; on the Internet at www.tfh.com; in CANADA Rolf C. Hagen Inc., 3225 Sartelon St. Laurent-Montreal Quebec H4R 1E8; Pet Trade by H & L Pet Supplies Inc., 27 Kingston Crescent, Kitchener, Ontario N2B 2T6; in ENGLAND by T.F.H. Publications, PO Box 15, Waterlooville PO7 6BQ; in AUSTRALIA AND THE SOUTH PACIFIC by T.F.H. (Australia), Pty. Ltd., Box 149, Brookvale 2100 N.S.W., Australia; in NEW ZEALAND by Brooklands Aquarium Ltd. 5 McGiven Drive, New Plymouth, RD1 New Zealand; in SOUTH AFRICA, Rolf C. Hagen S.A. (PTY.) LTD. P.O. Box 201199, Durban North 4016, South Africa; in Japan by T.F.H. Publications, Japan—Jiro Tsuda, 10-12-3 Ohjidai, Sakura, Chiba 285, Japan. Published by T.F.H. Publications, Inc.
MANUFACTURED IN THE
UNITED STATES OF AMERICA
BY T.F.H. PUBLICATIONS, INC.

Contents

Acknowledgments

I need to give a big "Thank You" to all of the following people for helping make this book possible. Each one has played a part in this project and has made my job a little easier and my life a little better.

Thanks to Garland and Betty, owners of Quality Pets, John, owner of Reef Creations, and Tim and Robbie, owner and employee of The Fish Bowl for letting me photograph every coral that came through their doors. Thanks to Nancy, former co-worker and neighbor, for teaching me a thing or two about corals and for also putting up with my shutterbug habits. And last, but not least, thanks to Mike, former employee of B&B Pet Stop, and Darin, former employee of Marine Warehouse Aquarium, for opening my eyes to the world of marine aquariums; and to Wade, owner of The Ideal Aquarium for simply giving me the encouragement to start my own career in the aquarium hobby and business when I needed it most. All of you should see a little of yourselves in this and every other aquarium book I have written and will write.

Photos by the author except as specifically noted otherwise.

At full size in the ocean or at mini-reef size in the home, the coral reefs are lands of enchantment and wonder, to be treasured and preserved as well as enjoyed and marveled at. Photo by Walt Deas.

The view above shows a reef exposed at low tide; the view below shows the submerged crest of a reef. The nations whose territories include such reefs are becoming increasingly stricter about the ground rules governing the behavior of visitors to the reefs. Photos by Walt Deas.

All About Stony, or Hard, Corals

THE NATURAL HISTORY OF STONY CORALS

The evolutionary history of corals began at a time when all life on Earth was very primitive and no organisms had yet developed a skeleton or any other significant hard body parts. In the ancient seas of the Precambrian Period, well over a half billion years ago, the rootstock of the biological group known as cnidarians (pronounced ny-dar-ree-ans; the "C" is silent) arose. The first cnidarians were soft-bodied organisms believed to be of close relation to modern jellyfish, but they eventually evolved into various different groups. Two of these later groups, the tabulates and the rugosans, acquired the ability to produce hard skeletons and thus were the first stony, or hard, corals. (The words "stony" and "hard" are both used interchangeably in reference to the corals we're discussing here, and the words are thus used interchangeably throughout this book.) Many were solitary corals, but a few did grow together in small colonies, leading to the formation of the first early coral reefs. These two groups went through many changes over a period of over 300 million years; then, at the end of the Permian Period, a global mass

Fossilized skeleton of an extinct rugose coral found in the Ordovician rocks of Ohio, making this specimen about 460 million years old. This particular type has the hallmark horn-shaped form of most rugosans. A few rugosans formed small colonies when individual skeletons grew together into clumps, but these structures were insignificant compared to today's tropical reefs.

A section of a very large (200 gallons) aquarium containing hard corals.

A piece of the fossilized skeleton of a tabulate coral found in Silurian rocks of Alabama, making this specimen around 420 million years old. All tabulates had a massive colonial form, many being similar to this piece in structure. Tabulates often formed small "patch reefs" that have been preserved in the fossil record, but even these reef structures were insignificant in size relative to those of today.

and provide a defense against attackers.

Cnidarians have no excretory system. All wastes are simply expelled through the mouth or are secreted through the body wall. Cnidarians also lack a respiratory system. Much-needed oxygen is absorbed through the body wall over the organism's entire surface. They don't have a central nervous system either. All that is present in most is a simple "nerve net."

Different corals can be found as individual animals

The basic structure of a jellyfish, a familiar free-swimming cnidarian. Drawing by John R. Quinn.

extinction occurred and both groups disappeared forever. Shortly after this extinction, in the early Triassic Period, the first relatives of modern stony corals appeared, and while it is not clear which one of the groups of cnidarians gave rise to these new corals, scientists have presented arguments that they evolved from either the rugosans or another group of cnidarians, the anemones. These stony corals, and all modern "true" hard corals, belong to the order Scleractinia. Since that time the scleractinians have been the predominant reef-building organisms in tropical marine waters around the world; they are represented by over 800 modern species.

THE ANATOMY OF STONY CORALS

When it comes to multicellular animals, only the sponges are simpler in design than the corals and their kin. Since their first

appearance they have remained relatively simple animals, and while they may take on many different forms, they are all very similar in basic design. All cnidarians have a very simple body wall that is divided into only two layers. The outer layer, which is comparable to the animal's skin, is called the ectodermis; the inner layer is called the endodermis, or gastrodermis. Also, between these two layers is a middle layer of a jelly-like substance called the mesoglea. Cnidarians have a mouth that opens into a single body cavity called the enteron, or gastrovascular cavity, where food enters and from which wastes are expelled. This mouth is also commonly surrounded by a ring of tentacles that help to capture and ingest food. If tentacles are present, they are usually covered by thousands of grappling and stinging cells called cnidocytes, which help to snare and neutralize food or as members of complex colonies. Each coral animal, whether as an individual or as part of a colony, is called a polyp, and each polyp has a mouth, a gastrovascular cavity, etc. Often in the colonial corals each polyp can be so well integrated with the surrounding polyps that it is practically impossible to tell where one polyp stops and

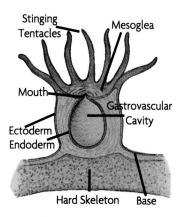

The basic structure of a stony coral. Individual coral animals are similar in some important anatomical regards to jellyfish and anemones but have the ability to build a hard skeleton.
Drawing by John R. Quinn.

another starts. In many of these corals the tissues are intimately connected and the colony lives as if it were one organism, sharing food and nutrients taken in and produced by each individual polyp.

Above: This button coral is a good example of a large solitary stony coral that builds a partially exposed skeleton.

Right: This staghorn coral is a good example of a colonial stony coral that has a branching skeleton and small polyps interconnected by a thin layer of tissue. Individual polyps are not easily discernible, and the living flesh of a colony typically looks more like a bumpy skin covering the skeleton. Each of the individual polyps can share nutrients with the rest of the colony.

Plate coral, a good example of a large solitary stony coral. It is an individual polyp with a single mouth and an internal skeleton.

CORAL FEEDING AND ALGAL SYMBIOSIS

Corals are more or less carnivorous, eating anything from the smallest plankton to relatively large fish. Corals that have relatively large tentacles often grab anything meaty that they can get a grip

This moon coral is a good example of a stony coral having a massive skeleton and large polyps that are interconnected by a thin layer of tissue. Each polyp is clearly distinguishable from its surrounding neighbors but can share nutrients with all of them. Such cooperation between polyps can be advantageous in some aspects but can also be a disadvantage if part of the colony is injured. If an injury occurs, disease can rapidly spread over the entire colony.

Trumpet coral, a good example of a colonial stony coral that has a branching skeleton and individual polyps. The end of each branch is built upon by a single polyp, which can eventually split in two and form two branches and two individual polyps. The colony as a whole grows as the polyps continue to split. It should be noted that each polyp can live or die without affecting the rest of the colony. Individual branches from such a coal can be broken away and used to start new colonies.

on, while many of the corals that do not have large tentacles, or have no obvious tentacles, are covered by a layer of mucus used to collect bacteria and plankton as if it were fly-paper. This mucous sheet is then "reeled in" to the mouth and then moved to the gastrovascular cavity, where the food is digested. Some corals use both of these methods of feeding. Ingested foods are first broken down in the gastrovascular cavity by enzymes and then are engulfed by cells in the endoderm. From there, nutrients are transported throughout the body while wastes are expelled through the mouth or are secreted directly through the body wall.

Many corals, especially stony corals, also receive nutrients from single-celled algae-like organisms that live in their tissues. These organisms are called zooxanthellae and are a type of dinoflagellate belonging to the genus *Symbiodinium*. This relationship between the coral and its zooxanthellae is called a symbiosis, meaning that both receive benefits from each other (as opposed to parasitism, where only one organism in the pairing receives benefits). The zooxanthellae provide the animals with oxygen, carbohydrates and a variety of other vital nutrients produced during photosynthesis; they also takes up some of the carbon dioxide produced by the coral during metabolism. In return, the coral provides the algae with a place to call home as well as a source of carbon dioxide, phosphate

and other required nutrients. It is also believed that through complex biochemical processes this symbiosis helps the coral to precipitate skeletal material at a faster rate than would otherwise be possible. This symbiotic relationship is why every time you've seen a picture of a coral reef it has been in shallow, clear, warm water. The zooxanthellae will survive if water temperatures stay between 64° and 87° F (preferably from 75° to 85° F) and need intense sunlight in order to carry out normal photosynthetic processes while deep inside the coral's tissues. For this reason symbiotic corals are almost always found at depths of less than 150 feet and are rarely found in waters deeper than 300 feet.

While many stony corals are carnivores that will capture and eat small zooplankton, crustaceans and fish, very few require being fed in a well lighted aquarium. In some cases, however, occasional feedings increase the overall size and growth rate of corals and if nothing else can be interesting to watch. Many corals can be fed brine shrimp through use of an eyedropper, while those with an especially potent sting can actually snare small live shrimp or feeder minnows. Small pieces of clam, squid and shrimp can be used as well. But since any food added to an aquarium increases the level of unwanted nutrients in the water, all such feedings should be made very sparingly, and any uneaten food should be removed very promptly.

Below: A plate coral enjoying a meal of brine shrimp given to it by means of a syringe.

THE WEAPONS OF STONY CORALS

Corals must compete for growing space on the reef and also attempt to protect themselves from predation. One of the basic weapons that corals employ to ensure survival are called acontia. These are extrudable digestive filaments that are normally kept inside the gastrovascular cavity. If something irritating or threatening comes into contact with many corals these filaments are pushed out through the mouth and actually secrete digestive substances onto whatever they touch. This is very effective for close-quarters fighting.

Many corals also have tentacles that surround the mouth or the perimeter of the body, and when present almost all are covered with cells that have the capacity to sting anything they touch. The particular cells that can sting are called cnidocytes. Cnidocytes have a complex mechanism called a

A hammer coral with extended sweeper tentacle. The exceptionally long tentacle hanging down (arrow) is a specialized stinging tentacle that can reach several inches farther than the "normal" tentacles and damage other corals nearby.

nematocyst that delivers the sting and they work like tiny barbed poisonous harpoons. They explode outward from the cnidocyte and inject a toxin into an attacker or into prey that they wish to capture and eat. Nematocysts are very sensitive to physical contact with an object, but also usually require chemical stimulation by an organic substance in order to "fire."

This keeps them from constantly firing every time they come into contact with non-threatening objects and non-prey items. Don't be scared, though. While the stings of various other cnidarians such as jellyfish and anemones are well known for their potency, most corals have such a weak sting that you can't even feel it through the thick skin on your hands!

A few of these corals have also have developed more specialized stinging tentacles that can stretch out to be much longer than the other "normal" tentacles. These extendable tentacles are called sweeper tentacles and are designed to be an offensive weapon against nearby neighbors on the reef. Sweeper tentacles sometimes reach lengths over half a foot and usually have a relatively strong sting that can severely damage or even kill other corals. This allows the coral to clear out an area around itself for future growth.

SKELETAL FORM OF STONY CORALS

Stony corals take in calcium from surrounding sea water and combine it with carbon dioxide taken from sea water and produced during metabolism to produce a calcium carbonate ($CaCO_3$) skeleton. Calcium carbonate is used by a variety of organisms from clams to starfish to create hard parts and in the coral's skeleton it is called aragonite. Aragonite is precipitated by each individual coral polyp whether it is solitary or part of a colony, and when large skeletons are produced by colonial corals the area where

A pearl bubble coral with numerous sweeper tentacles extending from between its water-filled vesicles.

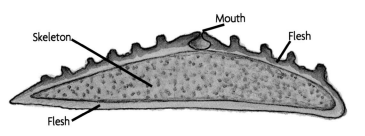

Cross-section of the flesh and skeleton of a plate coral, a solitary stony coral polyp.

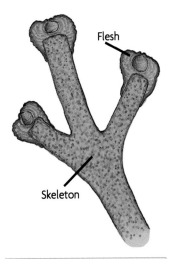

Cross-section of the flesh and skeleton of a trumpet coral, a branching colonial stony coral with separate polyps.

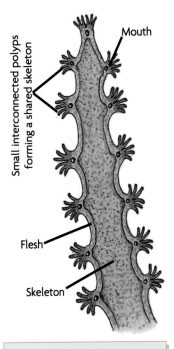

Cross-section of the flesh and skeleton of a staghorn coral, a branching colonial stony coral having interconnected polyps.

each polyp lays down aragonite is called a corallite.

The overall shape of the skeleton is developed according to selective forces in the reef environment, where body surface area is very important for individual survival and the proliferation of a species. Symbiotic corals must have the greatest amount of their bodies exposed to sunlight as possible in order to increase in size and to reproduce. Increased surface area also aids in the collection of bacteria and other prey and allows a greater potential for gas exchange across the body's ectoderm. However, their skeletons must also be able to weather water currents of various force depending on their physical location. In general, corals that live in areas where periodically very strong water currents or large storm waves may come upon them tend to have compact boulder-like skeletons that are very heavy and resistant to any sort of breakage. These skeletons have very little flesh compared

Cross-section of flesh and skeleton of a moon coral, a massive colonial stony coral with interconnected polyps.

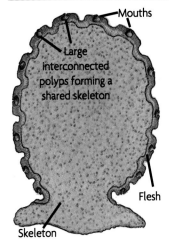

Cross-section of the flesh and skeleton of a button coral, a common solitary stony coral polyp.

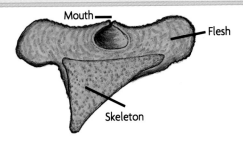

All drawings this page by John R. Quinn.

to the amount of skeleton produced and thus grow very slowly. Corals that live in areas where moderate currents or waves prevail typically have a more open form made of a few heavy branches. This form allows for the spreading out of the surface of the flesh over a greater area while still being strong enough to resist breakage and also allows for faster growth due to a higher flesh-to-skeleton ratio. Likewise, corals that live in areas where currents are moderate or lower and wave activity is at a minimum tend to have more finely branching and more open skeletons that further increase surface area and allow for even faster growth. Other types of corals that have large fleshy bodies with relatively small skeletons also will usually be found in areas of lower current and wave activity where their flesh will not be subject to tearing or other damage. Keep in mind, however, that what is considered to be a weak to moderate current on the reef may be considered strong to very strong in an aquarium.

This restriction to certain current or wave energy regimes is the primary factor that keeps various species of corals from living in more than one part of the reef environment. However, there are a few groups or species of corals that can actually vary the shape of their skeleton from individual to individual as needed in order to fit in just about anywhere on the reef. These corals will take on a massive structure in high current areas but if conditions on the reef change for some reason and currents and

waves become less powerful the corals will develop branching skeletons when producing new skeleton. This change is somewhat reversible and can often be observed when moving certain corals into an aquarium where the conditions are almost certainly different from those where the coral was collected. It is common to see a short, stubby-branched acropora that was collected in a high current area grow new longer and thinner branches when placed in an aquarium without a strong direct current. This ability to grow in a variety of forms also makes the identification of several species and different members of those species of corals very difficult.

CORAL REPRODUCTION

Corals reproduce sexually and asexually a number of different ways. Most corals are hermaphrodites having the ability to produce both eggs and sperm. Many of these corals can produce and eject eggs and sperm directly into surrounding waters where they will hopefully run into each other and those of their neighbors to produce juvenille corals called planulae. This method of sexual reproduction allows the coral's offspring to spread over a wider geographic range and allows a certain degree of genetic variabilty which is required in order to adapt to any environmental changes through natural selection. However, it also requires the coral to use a considerable amount of energy to produce sperm and eggs and thus is not always the best method of reproduction. Some other

It has become common for hobbyists to purposely fragment a few types of small-polyp corals like the acroporas and velvet corals. The technique is simple and allows the hobbyist to spread pieces of a larger colony to several new locations in an aquarium and to move pieces into other tanks. The operation consists of carefully breaking away one or more of the branches of an existing colony and using an underwater epoxy glue to permanently attach those fragments to a piece of live rock or dead coral or other suitable substrate. The epoxy glue hardens quickly and is not toxic to the fragments or anything else in the aquarium. Under optimal conditions each fragment quickly starts to grow and form a new base, eventually covering the adhesive and continuing to grow into a larger colony.

A specimen of acropora coral taken from a larger colony and attached to a clam shell with epoxy glue. Under good conditions the fragment will soon begin to grow upward and will also spread outward to cover the epoxy base.

The cone-shaped skeleton of a small bubble coral.

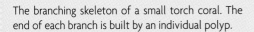

The branching skeleton of a small torch coral. The end of each branch is built by an individual polyp.

Cone-shaped skeleton of a medium-size elegance coral. Not all elegance corals share this skeletal form; some have a thinner and taller skeletal form.

The meandering skeleton of a large hammer coral.

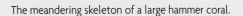

Skeleton of a short-tentacle plate coral.

Skeleton of a galaxy coral.

The branching skeleton of an acropora coral.

Above: Skeleton of a cauliflower coral. The thick branches ending in rounded knobs give this coral its common name.

Right: Skeleton of a typical horn coral, showing its thick branches and relatively tall form.

Below: Closeup of the skeleton of a ridge coral; the name obviously derives from the numerous small ridges covering the entire skeleton.

corals are brooders that undergo internal self-fertilization. After self-fertilization the parent also holds the planulae internally for some period of time and then releases them into the surrounding waters. This method of reproduction provides the planulae with a "head start" but also requires a considerable amount of energy and does not provide a means of genetic variation. Both of these methods of sexual reproduction commonly occur at specific time intervals or at a specific time of year usually related to lunar cycles or seasonal water temperature changes.

Far more common among corals is asexual reproduction where neither sperm nor eggs are produced. Corals can produce "buds" that grow from the parent and eventually get big enough to tear away and form a new individual or colony. Other corals reproduce asexually unintentionally through fragmentation. This is especially common among the less fleshy colonial stony corals, which are sometimes broken apart by storm activity and predation by coral-eating fishes. When large or small pieces of skeleton and tissue are broken away from the parent many have the ability to settle on the bottom and once again form new colonies.

THE TAXONOMY OF CNIDARIANS

The outline accompanying is a summary of the classification of modern cnidarians which shows how each group is related to the others. Cnidarian taxonomy is based on several characters

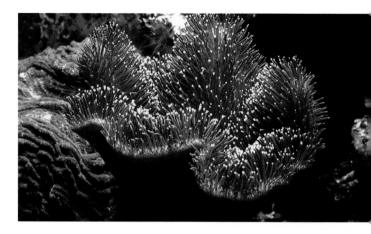

Above: Toadstool corals, sufficiently different from true stony corals (order Scleractinia) to be placed in the order Alcyonacea, which contains the cnidarians popularly referred to as soft corals or leather corals. They come in a wide variety of forms and colors.

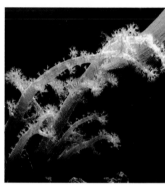

Above Right: A finger leather coral, closely related to the toadstool corals above but obviously very different in appearance. The entire phylum of cnidarians is characterized by look-alike confusions between animals that superficially resemble each other closely but are not placed taxonomically even within the same class.

These sun polyps (left) and daisy polyps (right) are zoanthids, members of an order (Zoanthidae) within the same subclass as the stony corals but more closely related to anemones than to corals.

Right: A jellyfish, like the stony corals a cnidarian but belonging to the class Scyphozoa, not Anthozoa. Photo by MP and C. Piednoir, Aqua Press.

Below: Hydroids (of the cnidarian class Hydrozoa) on a reef in the Philippines. Hydrozoans share with the jellyfishes the distinction of being among the most dangerous-to-man coelenterates. Photo by MP and C. Piednoir, Aqua Press.

Left: The anemone *Tealia piscivora*, one of the "true" anemones of the order Actiniaria, as opposed to the zoanthids and cerianthids, which certainly look like anemones.

Below: *Pachycerianthus forreyi*, a burrowing, or tube, anemone of the order Cerantharia. The burrowing anemones are different from true anemones to the degree that some systematists place them in their own subclass within the class Anthozoa.

A view of the polyps of *Tubipora,* a living organ pipe "coral." The organ pipes are members of the order Stolonifera, more closely related to the gorgonians and soft corals than to the true hard corals of the order Scleractinia.

These gorgonian animals, imaginatively and fairly accurately named sea whips, are typical members of the order Gorgonacea. Like the organ pipe corals they are more closely related to the soft corals than to the hard corals.

Mushroom anemones, order Corallimorpharia, more closely related to the true anemones (and to the true corals) than their superficial appearance would indicate.

Recreating the Reef Environment

In order to keep stony corals alive and well in an aquarium you must attempt to recreate their natural environment as closely as possible. That primarily consists of maintaining the water quality and providing the proper lighting to promote photosynthesis by zooxanthellae. The addition of various chemical supplements is also critical to your success. It should be noted that while much of the information that follows is pertinent to all marine aquariums, much is specifically aimed at the care of hard corals and is therefore very important to the reef hobbyist.

TEMPERATURE AND SPECIFIC GRAVITY

The water temperature around most coral reefs fluctuates between 70° and 85°F throughout the course of a year and is even more stable in many areas. So the water temperature of your reef aquarium also should stay within this range. However, because dissolved oxygen levels in aquarium water can drop significantly as temperature increases, it is best to keep the temperature closer to the lower side of the range than to the higher. Temperatures a little above 80°F are tolerable, but a temperature closer to 75°F is optimal. You should also keep in mind that while water temperatures fluctuate several degrees around reefs, the fluctuation usually takes place very slowly. The temperature may vary much less than one degree per month as seasons change. Therefore the water temperature of your aquarium should be kept as stable as possible as well as within the given range.

Quality submersible heaters with adjustable thermostats may be needed to keep temperatures up during winter months, but in most cases the aquarium will need to be cooled down rather than heated up. This is due to the excessive heat produced by most high-output lighting systems used for keeping reef aquariums. If this is the case, fans may be used to cool light bulbs and can also be positioned to blow across the surface of the aquarium water. The air stream from the fan promotes the rapid evaporation of water, which in turn cools the water left behind. This usually is sufficient, but in extreme cases it may be necessary to buy a water chiller made specifically for the job. These chillers are basically small refrigerators made so that water can be pumped through them and cooled. Unfortunately, they are usually rather expensive.

Specific gravity is a common way to measure the "saltiness" of water by comparing the weight of a given volume of water to the weight of an equal volume of pure fresh water having the same temperature. As a reference point pure water at room temperature has a specific gravity of 1.000. Therefore, an equal volume of water with any dissolved salts or other chemicals in it will be at least slightly heavier and thus will have a higher specific gravity than pure water. The specific gravity of seawater around most coral reefs varies from about 1.022 to 1.030 at 75°F. However, as water is made saltier and the specific gravity gets higher, the dissolved oxygen content of the water gets lower (it may be easier to think of the water as being "full of salt" and not leaving much room for oxygen and other gases to dissolve into it). For this reason it is best to keep the specific gravity in your aquarium closer to the lower limit of 1.022 in order to keep oxygen levels as high as possible.

Specific gravity is controlled best when making up artificial sea water to fill the aquarium and can easily be measured using a hydrometer. Note that once the aquarium has been filled with water of a certain specific gravity the only thing that will change that specific gravity is the evaporation of water (unless you add more salt later). As evaporation occurs, only pure water vapor escapes; the salts are left behind, thus slightly raising the specific gravity of the remaining water (That's why you should never forget to replace evaporated water with fresh water, not salt water!)

Above: Reef aquariums do not necessarily have to be extra-large. This photo shows a section of the reef scene in a 30-gallon tank.

Below: Part of a custom-built acrylic aquarium of about 60 gallons.

pH AND ALKALINITY

The pH of water—that is, its characterization as being acidic, neutral or basic— is expressed in a number on a scale ranging from 0 to14. The numbers are logarithmic representations, so each integer upward or downward represents a factor of 10. That is, water measured to be pH 5 is ten times more acidic than water of pH 6. Pure water, which is neutral, has a pH of 7. Water with a lower pH is acidic, and water with a higher pH is basic. Stony corals require that the pH in the aquarium be somewhat basic, and it has been observed that most stony corals can tolerate a range of from about 7.6 to 9.0. However, the pH of sea water around most coral reefs varies only from 8.0 to 8.4. For this reason it is best to maintain a pH in your aquarium that stays within this range.

The pH of aquarium water is primarily controlled by the concentration of dissolved carbon dioxide. If CO_2 concentrations are high the pH goes down, and when CO_2 concentrations are low the pH rises. It is thus best to keep CO_2 concentrations relatively low. This is usually accomplished in marine aquariums simply by maintaining good water circulation and by keeping the water's surface well agitated to promote good gas exchange between the aquarium and the atmosphere. If this does not keep the pH within acceptable limits the pH can be corrected by using any of a variety of buffers that can be purchased as powders or liquids. Just remember that if you must manually adjust the pH of your aquarium it must be done slowly, over a period of several hours, so that no corals are subjected to a "pH shock."

The alkalinity of water can be said to be a measure of how well it resists rapid changes in pH. As stated, the pH in an aquarium is strongly affected by the concentration of CO_2 in the water. Symbiotic algae inside corals use much of this CO_2 during the day, but at night photosynthesis stops and CO_2 concentrations go up. If the alkalinity is low, the pH commonly fluctuates a good bit from day to night. Various other conditions that change over time can also have an affect on pH changes. Any rapid pH swings are very detrimental to the health of hard corals (and many other organisms), thus requiring that the alkalinity be kept within acceptable limits. There are two basic scales used for expressing alkalinity measurements, with values given in milliequivalents per liter (meq/l) or in carbonate hardness (dKH). For sea water around most coral reefs the alkalinity ranges from 2.1 to 2.5 meq/l, or about 6 to 7 dKH. However, because aquariums tend to be by nature more unstable than the ocean, the optimum alkalinity should be maintained a little higher than that of sea water. Stony corals stay healthier and produce skeleton more quickly when an alkalinity between 2.5 and 3.5 meq/l (7-10 dKH) is maintained. Unfortunately, over time alkalinity will usually drop below acceptable levels if it is not maintained through the addition of alkalinity buffers, so it must be monitored and adjusted as often as necessary.

ESSENTIAL ELEMENTS

Several substances found in sea water are required by stony corals. They all must be added to the aquarium and if possible should be monitored regularly in order to ensure that they are maintained at acceptable levels.

Calcium

Stony corals must take in calcium from sea water for use in the precipitation of their calcium carbonate skeletons. On the reef ambient calcium concentrations are relatively high, at about 375 to 475 mg/l, compared to the concentrations of many other elements. Similar levels should be maintained in the aquarium, optimally nearer the upper limit of 475 mg/l. There are three basic ways to keep calcium levels this high. The first is by using liquid calcium additives. The most common types of liquid calcium additives are simply measured out according to the manufacturer's directions and added directly to the aquarium, typically on a weekly basis. They are thus very easy to use and are hard to overdose. However, they are usually made by binding the calcium to an organic base that is left over after the calcium has been released and utilized. Over time this can lead to an accumulation of unwanted organic material in the aquarium unless it is controlled by using an efficient protein skimmer. There also are newer liquid additives that come in two

Corals are not the only reef aquarium inhabitants that depend on the addition of a variety of additives. Tridacnid clams (right) and coralline algae (above) also depend on them, as do snails and certain other invertebrates.

parts. These additives require you to add a first part to the aquarium, wait a given amount of time, then add the second component.

A second method is the use of lime water, commonly called "kalkwasser." This is a liquid solution made by adding powdered calcium hydroxide to fresh water. This should be done according to the manufacturer's directions, which are basically the same no matter the brand. Basically, a small amount of the powder is added to a bucket of fresh water and stirred vigorously. The solution is then allowed to rest for several hours so that any of the undissolved white powder settles to the bottom. Then the top portion of the solution is poured into the aquarium, leaving behind the milky portion that forms in the bottom. However, care must be taken to add the solution very slowly to the aquarium in an area of high water flow or the solution can cause unwanted rapid pH changes. This method sounds like a lot of trouble compared to using prefabricated additives, but it has benefits that the additives don't. The chemistry of the lime water solution when combined with aquarium water helps to maintain a high pH and high alkalinity levels when used correctly. These are very desirable side-effects that are not seen with the use of liquid additives, and they make the extra work well worth it.

The third method is the use of a device called a calcium reactor. These devices add calcium to the aquarium water by dissolving calcium carbonate. This is done by injecting CO_2 (from a pressurized bottle) into the reactor, which is filled with crushed aragonite sand. This creates a low pH within the reactor, which in turn causes the sand to very slowly dissolve into the aquarium water. Calcium reactors are complicated-looking contraptions and are usually somewhat expensive, but they are actually quite simple to use and are very effective.

Strontium

Stony corals also add strontium into their skeletons during the precipitation of aragonite; apparently, they can't thrive without it. Strontium is found at concentrations of 8 to 10 mg/l in sea water and thus should be maintained at about the same levels in the aquarium. There are several good prefabricated strontium additives available to hobbyists; they should be used according to the manufacturer's directions. Also, if a calcium reactor is used there is no need for this additive. Strontium levels will be maintained because strontium is released with calcium as aragonite is dissolved within the reactor. Unfortunately, unlike calcium levels and many other water parameters, strontium levels cannot be easily verified by hobbyists. It seems that no one has yet developed a simple (or maybe just affordable) method of accurately measuring strontium levels in aquarium water. So if you use additives be sure to follow directions and watch for signs of decreased calcification that may be due to a strontium deficiency.

Iodine

While normally we all think of oxygen as being a good thing, it is produced in different forms during photosynthetic and metabolic processes within the coral. Some forms can be very destructive and must be neutralized within the coral's tissues in order to avoid problematic levels. To combat this potential toxic buildup, stony corals use iodine in complex processes to neutralize these destructive forms of oxygen, making iodine another required element. Iodine is found in several forms in sea water at a concentration of about 60 parts per billion and can be added to the aquarium by using any of a wide variety of prefabricated liquid additives. Again, it is best to simply follow the manufacturer's directions for any of them.

Trace Elements

Several other elements found in very low concentrations in sea water are nevertheless important in the maintenance of hard corals. However, because the term "trace elements" includes several different individual elements found in very low concentrations, it is not practical to test their concentrations in aquarium water. But most are found in quality salt mixes and can be maintained in sufficient concentrations even if only small water changes are performed regularly. There are also several trace element additives available in liquid form and in blocks that slowly dissolve over a period of days or weeks when placed in the aquarium.

Phosphates

While tiny amounts of phosphate are required by corals, there is basically never any need to add any to the aquarium. In fact, almost without exception reef aquariums have much higher than desirable levels of phosphate, and the hobbyist must constantly try to keep concentrations at a minimum. This is because various forms of phosphate can cause real problems in the aquarium if levels rise to concentrations even as low as 0.1ppm. Monitoring the concentration

The population of fishes in general in a reef aquarium should be kept to a minimum because they have to be fed and therefore have a tendency to cause a buildup of phosphates; additionally, certain groups of fishes should be avoided entirely because they eat coral polyps. The butterflyfishes (*Chaetodon quadrimaculatus* shown here) are one such group. Photo by Mark Smith.

of phosphate in the aquarium is somewhat troublesome to hobbyists, because it is very difficult to test. Unfortunately, phosphate comes in organic and inorganic forms, and most test kits can only measure the inorganic type. You must do what you can to keep inorganic phosphate below 0.1ppm, the closer to zero the better. Even very low concentrations of phosphate promote the growth of unwanted algae and can interfere with the precipitation of aragonite skeletal material. When phosphate levels are too high a coral's fleshy parts may continue to grow, but the skeleton will not grow, as the phosphate has a poisoning effect on precipitation chemistry. This condition can lead to serious health problems for the coral and commonly causes the coral to separate from its skeleton and die.

Phosphate concentrations commonly are high in tap water, so it is almost always best to use purified water when replacing evaporated aquarium water and when doing water changes. Phosphate also enters the aquarium as an integral part of fish foods, which is a good reason to keep fish populations at a minimum in a reef aquarium. Even if there are only a few fish in your aquarium you should still be very cautious about overfeeding them. If phosphate is still a problem there are several products that are made to absorb and remove phosphate from the water. Most of them work very well, but they can be somewhat expensive if used on a continual basis.

ORGANIC COMPOUNDS AND OTHER IMPURITIES

The removal of surplus organic materials and other unwanted chemicals is also very important. In most aquariums this is usually carried out by using activated carbon as a chemical "sponge" because it has the ability to absorb quite a variety of these compounds. However, activated carbon also sucks up many of the chemicals required by corals to live, so it should not be used frequently in reef aquariums. Carbon should instead be used periodically, maybe for a few days every two or three months. Specialized filters called protein skimmers are used instead. Protein skimmers, which are almost always tubular devices, produce a thick foam internally that can be collected and discarded. There are two basic types of skimmers, venturi-driven and airstone-driven, but both make a foam by means of producing thousands of tiny air bubbles that are forced into the aquarium water,

a 60-gallon cube-shaped aquarium equipped with a protein skimmer, visible at the rear of the tank.

which is run through the skimmer by means of an external pump or powerhead. Many organic molecules, oils, detergents, etc., have a natural tendency to adhere to the surface of the bubbles and thus can be extracted from the aquarium water by removing the foam. They also aid in the lessening or removal of nitrate and phosphates as well and are a vital piece of equipment in the maintenance of high water quality. You should definitely invest in a well made model that is rated for the size of your aquarium.

AMMONIA, NITRITE AND NITRATE

It is well known that fish and other organisms in marine aquaria excrete highly toxic ammonia as a waste product of their metabolism. Ammonia is also produced in the aquarium by the decay and breakdown of fish foods, organic matter and dead tissues, and it can sometimes be found in tap water. Fortunately, two types of bacteria will establish themselves in an aquarium and will convert ammonia to other chemicals. This is done by *Nitrosomonas* bacteria, which use ammonia as a food source and convert it into nitrite (which is also toxic). Next, *Nitrobacter* bacteria use the nitrite for food and convert it to the far, far less toxic compound nitrate. This conversion is commonly known as the nitrogen cycle and is the goal of "biological filtration."

In the sea water around coral reefs, ammonia and nitrite levels are effectively non-existent, because they are used up as quickly as they are produced. Therefore, the concentration of both ammonia and nitrite in the aquarium should always be zero (0 ppm). Special biological filters must be used on most marine (and freshwater) aquariums to provide a place for these bacteria to live and multiply in order to reach such an equilibrium. They come in many shapes and sizes, the most common being wet-dry filters, undergravel filters and fluidized-bed filters. However, bacteria will also grow on and in the rough natural surfaces of live rock. Therefore, in reef aquariums that have a sufficient amount of live rock, none of these biological filters are required. The exact amount of live rock needed is highly variable, depending on how much livestock is added to the aquarium, but somewhere from 1 to 2 pounds of rock per gallon of aquarium volume is usually more than sufficient. If much less rock than this is used in the aquarium, or if the aquarium is very well stocked with fish, additional biological filtration may be needed.

After setting up a marine aquarium there is usually a 3-week to 5-week period of waiting for the bacteria to multiply and colonize the biological filter. This wait is called the "cycling period" and is normally accompanied by adding one or two small fish to the aquarium and nothing else for a while. The fish carry some of the bacteria, which will slowly begin to consume the toxins that the fish excrete and will multiply until an equilibrium is reached between ammonia production and consumption. The bacteria are normally slow to multiply, which is why the wait is so long. If live rock is added to a marine aquarium when it is being set up, the waiting period is typically much shorter, the reason being that the rock may already be heavily colonized with bacteria. So remember that if you use plenty of live rock you might not need extra biological filters such as wet-drys, and the time it takes to cycle the aquarium will probably be relatively short. However, no matter how you get started you should always try to consult knowledgeable aquarium shop staff or hobbyists and use the appropriate test kits to determine whether it is safe to begin adding corals to your aquarium.

After all of this is done you are still stuck with the nitrate produced by the *Nitrobacter* bacteria. There are varieties of bacteria that use nitrate for food, but they are a different type of bacteria and can thrive only in water with very little or no dissolved oxygen. For this reason nitrate is consumed bacterially only deep within the tiny pores and cracks found in pieces of live rock, where oxygen levels are lower than in the rest of the aquarium. It is also why nitrate is usually produced faster than it is used up.

Excess nitrate apparently does not have any direct toxic effect on most aquarium inhabitants, but it does have a long-term effect on the pH and alkalinity in the aquarium. This is due to the fact that nitrate in the aquarium leads to the production of small amounts of nitric acid, which lowers pH. Periodic partial water changes can reduce the concentration of nitrate if it should become a problem, and protein skimmers can help reduce levels as well.

WATER CLARITY

Aquarium water is usually made cloudy by suspended particles of various sorts that are produced within the aquarium. These particles include feces (whole or broken up), fish foods, dead microorganisms and silt/sediment produced by the natural breakdown of rocks in the aquarium caused by boring and burrowing organisms. So, other than using live rock for biological filtration and skimmers for chemical filtration, the only other filter needed is a mechanical filter to remove these particles from the aquarium and keep the water clear. Of course, "mechanical" filters also do a certain amount of biological filtration once beneficial bacteria have become established within them, and they can also be equipped to provide chemical filtration as well; it is just that they remain primarily mechanical.

Several types of mechanical filters on the market use a variety of filter media that can be either cleaned or replaced once they become soiled. One of the most common types of mechanical filter is the outside power filter that hangs off the back of the aquarium and typically contains filter floss, pads or sponges. Many models also come with activated carbon in small bags or in bonded pads and allow room for the addition of a small bag of phosphate remover when needed. Canister filters are another popular type of filter. Typically constructed from a cylinder with a self-contained pump and filter media, they can provide mechanical or biological or chemical filtration according to the way they're set up and used. Canister filters are more appealing to some hobbyists because they usually sit out of sight underneath the aquarium and allow the aquarium to be placed very close to the wall. Many of these filters have specialized baskets or compartments for holding filter floss or sponges and will also hold activated carbon or phosphate remover.

LIGHTING SPECTRUM AND INTENSITY

Lighting is the basic and most important (and commonly the most expensive) difference between the "fish-only" marine aquarium and the reef aquarium. Because almost all of the corals that we put into aquariums have photosynthetic zooxanthellae, most require special lighting systems that emit intense light over particular parts of the spectrum. It is therefore vital to purchase a lighting system that produces light of this quality and is sufficiently bright for any corals you wish to keep.

Water acts as something of a filter that cuts out the red and yellow parts of the spectrum in the first few feet of depth, which is why waters around coral reefs always have a blue color to them unless the water is very shallow. Zooxanthellae have

These photos of the same tank scene clearly show the difference in types of lighting. The photo above shows the scene under actinic lighting alone, and the photo below shows the same scene under halide lighting (5500 K bulbs) alone. Combinations of the two types provide the spectrum closest to natural conditions on the reef.

adapted to this situation by being able to specifically use blue light for photosynthetic processes. Therefore the basic idea is to use lights that emit a sufficient amount of blue light to promote photosynthesis. However, a certain amount of white light is also usually desirable over the aquarium so that it doesn't look as if it is full of toilet tank freshener.

The color of any light can be described in degrees Kelvin (°K). The more towards the yellow and red part of the spectrum the lower the Kelvin number, and the more towards the blue part the higher the number. While yellowish street lights are usually 4,700°K, actinic (blue-producing) bulbs are around 7,100°K. The optimum color lighting for reef aquariums is around the same as normal daylight or a little bluer, so you should use a lighting system that produces a bright light that is about 6,500°K to 6,800°K.

This can be done in two basic ways. The first and easiest way is to simply buy bulbs that emit light at 6,500°K to 6,800°K. Some metal halide bulbs currently on the market emit light at exactly 6,500°K, and there are also several brands of fluorescent bulbs that are a mixture of both white and blue light and are appropriately called 50/50 or daylight bulbs. The overall color of these bulbs is usually just a little bluer than daylight and is thus ideal for reef aquariums. The other approach is to use a combination of bulbs of various colors that produce an overall emission similar to

Looking into an activated lighting system consisting of a combination of two 6500 K metal halide bulbs and two VHO actinic bulbs. This particular system comes pre-mounted in a wooden canopy that includes an internal reflector, a protective sheet of acrylic, and two cooling fans.

A 48-inch Very High Output retrofitted lighting system designed for use with a 75-gallon reef aquarium in an aquarium store. This system uses a combination of two daylight bulbs and two actinic bulbs and has sufficient output to keep most corals alive and well. The heat given off by the system is low enough that by using a canopy with an open back the need for cooling fans has been avoided.

A power compact lighting system that uses a combination of daylight and actinic bulbs. Each of the two bulbs has two separate interconnected tubes and one base. (The appearance of more bulbs is caused by mirrored images in the reflector built into the unit.) This unit generates a good deal of heat but is equipped with a fan to dissipate the heat. The unit is shown here unactivated and activated.

daylight. This is commonly done by using metal halide bulbs that are 5,500°K with fluorescent bulbs that are 7,100°K. While it is not necessary, many hobbyists also prefer their lighting to actually be even bluer. This is

also easily done by combining fluorescent bulbs that are 7,100°K or metal halide bulbs that are 10,000°K with fluorescent bulbs that are 6,500°K.

The other basic consideration is intensity. The

ight spectrum means little if
he intensity is too low.
Regular wattage fluorescent
bulbs come in a variety of
colors from white to actinic-
white (50/50) to actinic.
However, these bulbs do not
have a very high output at all
compared with high output
(HO) and very high output
(VHO) bulbs —but they are
much less expensive. While a
few corals can survive with
several of these bulbs over the
aquarium, most will require
more intense lighting in order
to survive more than a few
months. High output and very
high output bulbs in these
colors are a big step up. While
a normal 4-foot fluorescent
bulb has an output of 40
watts, a 4-foot HO bulb puts
out around 85 watts, and a 4-
foot VHO bulb puts out
around 110 watts. Three or
four of these bulbs over a
tank that is less than about 2
feet deep are sufficient to
successfully keep many types
of stony corals. Power
compact bulbs are another
type of fluorescent lighting;
relatively new to the market,
they also have a much higher
output than regular wattage
bulbs and are actually a bit
brighter than HO and VHO
bulbs. Metal halides are by a
long shot the most intense
lights available for aquarium
applications. They are large
bulbs that look just like
streetlight bulbs. They also
come in a variety of spectra,
from 4,500°K up to 20,000°K.
However, the 5,500°K and
6500°K varieties seem to be
not only the most reliable but
also the cheapest, and as
discussed when used in
combination with actinic
fluorescent bulbs they provide
a very desirable spectrum.

A necessary feature in VHO electronic units that serve as power sources for
fluorescent aquarium lamps is that their circuitry be protected from humidity
and direct water contact; being fan-cooled is an added advantage.
Photo courtesy of Ultra Life Reef Products.

Unfortunately, the brighter
a particular type of bulb is,
the more it usually costs and
the more the fixtures and
ballasts cost as well. Most
manufacturers and hobbyists
suggest replacing bulbs every
9 to 18 months depending on
the type, so keep in mind the
cost of replacing all of your
bulbs when deciding on a
lighting system. Many of the
more intense lighting systems
will also get so hot that
special cooling fans must be
mounted in the canopy or
fixture to keep the
temperature down.
When it comes to how
much lighting your aquarium
needs, keep in mind that the
vast majority of stony corals
need at least moderate (HO/
VHO/power compact) to
intense (metal halide) lighting.
For the most part you should
try to have the greatest
number of bulbs that you can

mount over your aquarium
without overheating the water
(and without breaking you).
It's practically impossible to
overdo it. Also keep in mind
that the deeper your tank is,
the less light reaches the
organisms nearer the bottom,
which means that in general
the deeper the tank, the more
lighting you'll need.
One more note: in order to
more closely reproduce
lighting conditions on the reef,
remember that if it is possible
only part of the lighting
system should be turned on
in the morning to simulate the
morning sun. All the lights
should come on during the
day to simulate strong
daylight, followed by having
part of the system turned off
in the early evening to
simulate the afternoon sun.
The total lighting time should
be around twelve hours per
day, just as it is on the reef.

Selecting Corals for Your Aquarium

SHOPPING FOR STONY CORALS

There are a few things that you should always take into consideration when shopping for corals. You must pay careful attention to whether or not certain corals are compatible with other corals you already have or plan to purchase in the future, whether or not certain corals will thrive in your aquarium with the lighting system that you have, etc. Information concerning these characteristics of various popular hard corals is provided in the next section.

Another important factor to take into account is the condition of an individual coral that is for sale. To ensure greater success with them, stony corals must be inspected carefully before any purchase is made. "Wild" corals are collected almost exclusively in the tropical waters of the South Pacific and are shipped all the way to your local aquarium shop. To do this, divers must go out onto the reef and carefully (sometimes not carefully enough) collect individual coral specimens. Some corals are free-living and are easily gathered, but others are firmly attached to the reef and must be broken away with hammers and chisels. Corals are then transported to a collection station where they are individually bagged, packed in Styrofoam and cardboard boxes, and driven to the local airport. From there most corals destined for use in the United States are

flown to California, usually Los Angeles, and from there are distributed nationwide. Some suppliers remove the corals from their bags and temporarily place them in holding tanks when they first arrive from the Pacific. The corals are then rebagged and reshipped when they are sold, but others simply rush the corals straight through to

At first glance this torch coral may look healthy, but under closer inspection it's clear that part of the individual polyp (at center of photo) is dying of tissue necrosis. Normally a coral showing signs of tissue necrosis should be avoided, but if only one polyp of a branching colony is affected it may be possible to simply break off the affected branch.

stores on the first available flight. The whole trip from collection to store usually takes *at least* 24 hours and often takes as long as 48 hours. Some corals may stay in holding tanks for several days before they are sold, and if conditions are not optimal the coral's health can rapidly decline. The environmental shock of being collected and

bagged, as well as the physical stress of flying (rough handling, rapid temperature changes, etc.) often means that when corals finally arrive at the store, many of them may not be in exactly great condition. For this reason when shopping for new corals you should always be on the lookout for and avoid:

Corals that have obvious tissue damage or recession

Tissue damage or decay is usually seen as areas of the coral's fleshy body that have a moldy or rotten look to them, often called tissue necrosis. Dead or damaged flesh is often covered by a nasty brown jelly-like material, while in other cases it is only evident as obvious missing areas of flesh where the coral's white skeleton shows prominently. This condition usually worsens over a short period of time and can lead to the death of an individual or sometimes a whole colony. An exception is in cases where a stony coral has a branching skeleton that is covered with multiple polyps that are not connected by flesh, but only by skeleton. If this is the case, the damaged or dead polyps can sometimes be carefully broken away or cut off without any damage to the rest of the colony.

Tissue recession is often related to tissue necrosis and is seen as areas where the coral's body has pulled away from the skeleton. This is usually very obvious, because the coral's white skeleton

This frogspawn coral has rotted away from tissue necrosis, a persistent degradation of its soft tissue, over a period of a few days. The exposed area of the skeleton has already been overgrown by algae, which can make any chance of recovery even more remote. Avoid corals that exhibit similar signs of trouble.

your aquarium, your best treatment is to take it out of the aquarium and put it into a bowl of fresh water (make sure the water has been dechlorinated) for five minutes or so. That puts a lot of stress on the coral, but it also will kill all of the protozoan attackers. The treatment may

An acropora coral suffering from tissue necrosis that started at the base and is rapidly advancing toward the tips of the branches. The lack of any algae on the exposed skeleton is an indication of just how quickly this condition can spread.

shows prominently for a short period and is then covered by microalgae. In other cases tissue recession is not caused by necrosis, and the polyp simply peels away from the skeleton with no apparent damage. This is commonly called white-band disease and in extreme cases is called polyp "bailout" when the entire polyp detaches itself from its skeleton and is carried away by currents undamaged. Unfortunately, the free-floating polyp will almost certainly die. Again, the exception is in cases where a stony coral has a branching skeleton that is covered with multiple polyps that are not connected by flesh, only by skeleton. If severe recession occurs with one or a few polyps, they may be carefully broken away or cut off without any damage to the rest of the colony.

When corals suffer from tissue necrosis they usually

will become covered with and infected by millions of protozoans. This infection causes what is called "brown jelly disease," which can completely wipe out a coral within 24 hours if conditions are right. If a coral develops brown jelly disease while in

A lettuce coral afflicted by tissue necrosis. On this specimen only the tips of a few of the branches have been affected, but the condition can spread rapidly and kill the entire colony.

seem extreme, but since most corals that develop brown jelly disease die quickly if left untreated, you might as well try something to save it. After the freshwater bath the coral can be placed back into the aquarium, preferably in an area in which strong currents blow over its surface, to help prevent any further buildup of the jelly. If possible, it also is

Already suffering from issue recession, this moon coral now has been colonized by bubble algae (*Valonia*). This alga can be very persistent and can spread quickly; it will inhibit the regrowth of coral tissue even if conditions for recovery are optimal. The algae should be cleaned off the coral outside the aquarium to prevent further spreading.

Closed brain coral suffering from severe tissue recession. Unlike tissue necrosis, recession usually takes weeks to become this advanced. The flesh of this coral covered the entire skeleton when it was purchased, but it has dwindled away over a period of about three months. Immediate corrective measures are required.

always better to place the coral in a separate hospital tank so that if it does die it can't foul the water in your reef aquarium.

Corals that suffer from tissue recession in the aquarium are usually victims of high phosphate levels, low strontium levels or low pH/alkalinity. All of these faults can greatly inhibit the precipitation of aragonite, which leads to the separation of the coral's flesh from the skeleton. If corals in your aquarium suffer from tissue recession, you should test your water quality and make any necessary adjustments to help resolve the problem. If levels are corrected promptly enough, corals will almost always make a speedy recovery if the condition was not too far advanced to begin with.

Corals that have broken skeletons

If a coral's skeleton shows obvious breakage it should be avoided, because where there is broken skeleton there is usually torn flesh. If this is the case the coral may succumb to complications from necrosis or recession. This is much more of a problem with large fleshy corals than small-polyped corals, which actually reproduce by fragmentation of their skeleton. It also is not a problem with corals that have branching skeletons in which the polyps are not connected by flesh.

Corals that have bleached

A bleached coral in effect has lost most or all of its zooxanthellae. This is a common side effect of the coral's getting too hot during shipping, but it can be caused by other factors such as exposure to excessive UV radiation or from a lack of intense light. In the wild they are sometimes repopulated by zooxanthellae relatively quickly and survive, but they typically do not recover in aquariums. In some cases only one or a few of the polyps of a branching colony may bleach, and if they are not connected to other polyps by flesh they may be broken away if they do not survive.

If a coral suffers from bleaching after it has been placed into the aquarium it is most commonly caused by inappropriate light intensity.

Corals can be "burned" by very intense lighting if they come from areas of a reef that are not as brightly lit as the aquaria into which they're placed. Like people, corals have protective pigments, but they take time to adjust to new conditions. Bleaching can also occur when a coral's placed into an area where it receives much less light than it received before it was collected. In this case it is thought that the coral expels

level. If it bleaches when at the bottom of the tank, try doing just the opposite by moving it first to the top and then slowly toward the bottom of the tank over a period of weeks.

Fleshy corals that are not expanded

Large-polyped stony corals usually absorb water into their tissues and swell up, expanding well beyond their skeleton. However, most all

Bleaching in a tooth coral caused by overheating during shipment. Avoid corals bleached to this extent.

An example of partial bleaching in a worm brain coral caused by improper placement in the aquarium. This coral should receive light from all sides but has been placed (above left) so that its bottom is constantly shadowed. When photographed while being illuminated with a flashlight (above right), it can be seen that the coral has lost the zooxanthellae in the shaded portion of the coral.

retract somewhat at night or when they are irritated or unhealthy. Most corals will be shrunken and retracted into their skeletons when they arrive, but if they are healthy they should begin to expand within a couple of days at the most. If after a few days the coral has not at least begun to expand it should not be purchased. When dealing with an aggressive coral it is also a good idea to wait and see just how much it will expand to make sure that you have enough room for it in your aquarium.

its zooxanthellae in hopes that a new strain, one that can thrive under light of low intensity, will inhabit its tissues. In either case, the best thing to do is to move the coral either up or down in the aquarium according to whether you think the coral is receiving too little or too much light. If it bleaches when it's at the top of the tank, move it to the bottom. If it then begins to recover, you should wait until it has regained its color and then move it a few inches at a time over a period of weeks until it is at the desired

A bleached trumpet coral that has expelled all of its zooxanthellae and has little chance for survival.

The Individual Corals

This section is intended to provide you with specific information about many of the stony corals commonly seen for sale in aquarium stores. While in the past it seemed as if every other supplier and retailer had made up their own names for each individual type of coral, today almost all have one somewhat universal common name. In the pages that follow, various corals are listed by those individual common names and by their scientific names as well. For those corals that are frequently still called by more than one common name, the other less frequently used name(s) are also listed to avoid any confusion.

When looking at scientific names, which all are given in *italic* letters, remember that the first name in the pair, which always starts with a capital letter, is the genus that the coral belongs to. The second name, which is not capitalized even if it is based on a proper noun, is the specific name, or specific epithet. Some corals that are very similar in appearance may share a common name but are actually members of different groups or are different species within the same genus. For these corals only the genus is given, followed by "spp." instead of listing off every individual species name.

For each coral or group of corals some basic information is given to explain a little about them and to help you choose which corals to stock your aquarium with. When it is needed, more specific information is also provided. For each coral or group of corals their general lighting and current requirements as well as their overall hardiness and degree of aggressiveness are given. However, you should keep in mind that these are general guidelines and are greatly dependent on the water quality in your aquarium and the dealer's aquariums, how various corals tolerate shipping at different times of the year, how and where they are collected and other factors.

Lighting Requirements

Various lighting systems are considered to be low output, moderate output, or intense output. For general purposes several regular wattage fluorescent bulbs (4 to 6) over aquariums from 18 to 24 inches deep (most aquariums from 55 to 150 gallons) is considered low output, even if actinic bulbs are included. Moderate lighting output over the same aquariums requires the use of several VHO fluorescent bulbs or power-compact bulbs. To achieve intense lighting over the same aquariums requires the use of metal halide systems, usually

A small bubble coral. It is easy to see how this coral derived its common name from the round water-filled vesicles covering its body.

with a combination of fluorescent bulbs. Of course you must keep in mind that a system that is considered to be moderate over an aquarium that is 20 inches deep would be considered intense over an aquarium only 12 inches deep and would be considered low over an aquarium that is 36 inches deep. The depth (distance from the bulbs) at which a coral is placed in the aquarium is affected the same way. A coral that requires only moderate lighting may thrive at the very bottom of a deep aquarium with an intense lighting system, whereas a coral that requires intense light may need to be placed very near the top of the aquarium. Try to use good common sense when choosing corals according to your own lighting system and where you plan on placing each coral.

Current Requirements

Current preferences are more straightforward. Many of the more fleshy corals, or corals that have delicate soft parts, prefer to be placed in areas of low current. They should be placed where there is little water movement or they commonly will not expand fully, in order to avoid injuries caused by tearing of their flesh. The majority of corals will do fine with a moderate current. They should be placed in an area where there is considerable water movement, but not in a direct current from a powerhead or other pump return. Lastly, corals that actually thrive in a strong current should be placed where they are directly blown upon by currents from powerheads or other pumps.

Closeup of a bubble coral showing the characteristic fingerprint-like pattern seen on the vesicles.

Overall Hardiness

Many corals are damaged or injured during collection and die during the trip to the pet store or shortly after. For this reason the information concerning the hardiness of different corals is a guide to how well they commonly fare in the aquarium if they are unharmed after shipping or if they go on to survive any problems. In other words, just because you might see a shipment of corals come in with several dead or dying individuals does not mean that those corals are particularly fragile or are not hardy. They may have simply had an unusually bad trip.

Aggressiveness

The aggressiveness of different corals is affected by several factors. Some corals are considered to be non-aggressive and can be placed very near, or even in direct contact with, other corals. In many cases you should be more worried about these corals being victims instead of aggressors. However, as discussed earlier, many other corals have stinging tentacles or acontia that can be employed in order to damage or kill neighboring corals. Some must come into direct contact with other corals to do any damage, while others have tentacles that can sting other corals within a few inches. Worse still are corals that have long sweeper tentacles that can reach out up to several inches and deliver strong stings. Remember that many corals also expand well beyond their skeleton, which increases their area of influence. To avoid problems caused by having corals stinging one another, it is always a good idea to try and figure out a coral's maximum expanded size before placing it into your aquarium.

CLASS ANTHOZOA
ORDER SCLERACTINIA
(True Stony Corals)

FAMILY CARYOPHYLLIIDAE
Bubble/Bladder Coral, *Plerogyra sinuosa*

Bubble corals are aptly named for the swollen balloon or bladder-like vesicles that cover their bodies during daylight hours. These vesicles are actually modified tentacles that are filled with water; they vary in size and shape from individual to individual and in some cases can reach a diameter of almost two inches. They are also found in several color varieties, from transparent white to pale brown or green, and oftentimes the vesicles are also covered by fine lines or darker patches of color. Bubble corals tend to be moderately hardy, but they may have a tendency to recede slightly from their skeletons. They prefer moderate to intense lighting

and a weak to moderate current. If the current is too strong it can damage the delicate bubbles and the coral will not fully expand, so it is best to keep the current at a minimum. Bubble corals also have very thin sweeper tentacles that are commonly an inch or two in length. These sweepers tend to elongate at night when the vesicles are shrunken; they can badly sting neighboring corals, so always give bubble corals a couple of inches of space.

Pearl Bubble Coral, *Plerogyra* spp.

Pearl bubble corals also are named for the balloon-like bubbles that cover their bodies. However, unlike the large ovoid tentacles of the "regular" bubble coral, the pearl bubbles have much smaller vesicles, many of which are covered with small protuberances. Pearl bubble corals tend to be moderately hardy but also may suffer from some degree of recession from the skeleton. Like their cousins they prefer moderate to intense lighting and a weak

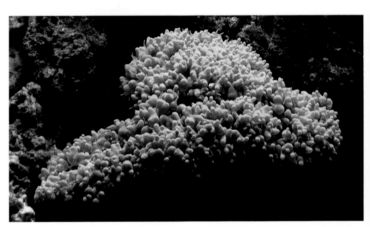

Closeup of a bubble coral showing its slender sweeper tentacles protruding from between the larger bubble-like vesicles.

A pearl bubble coral. Notice the difference between the knobby vesicles of this pearl bubble coral and the smooth vesicles of its cousin the bubble coral.

to moderate current. Pearl bubble corals also have potent sweeper tentacles that are commonly and inch or two in length, thus they will need to be given a couple of inches of space from other corals. One interesting exception is that different members of the genus *Plerogyra* do not sting each other, making it safe to place a bubble coral in direct contact with a pearl bubble coral.

A pearl bubble coral in closeup, showing the difference between the swollen sac-like modified tentacles and the thin sweeper tentacles it commonly uses to capture small crustaceans for food and to sting other corals.

capture and eat relatively large prey, including live fish. The tentacles are extended during the day and at night, and the coral is usually a combination of green, gray, pink, brown or purple and is very fleshy (hence the name meat coral). They do not have sweeper tentacles, but their ability to expand several inches beyond their skeleton makes them dangerous to neighboring corals that can be killed rather quickly. Elegance corals do well under moderate

Elegance/Meat Coral,
Catalaphyllia jardinei

Elegance corals are large solitary corals that are usually quite hardy and do very well in aquariums if they survive shipping without any tissue damage. In fact, under optimal conditions elegance corals will expand to a much larger size in an aquarium than they often do in the wild. They are also one of the few corals that can actually give you an annoying sting on the hand if not carefully handled by the skeleton. They can use their powerful stings to

Another example of an elegance coral. Individuals of this species vary greatly in colors and tentacle lengths according to the locality in which they're found.

An elegance coral looking nicely elegant as it waves its tentacles in the current.

to intense lighting but can also tolerate lower lighting conditions, often being found in cloudy, turbid waters in the wild. They also prefer a low to moderate current in which they can fully expand.

Fox Coral, *Nemezophyllia turbida*

It seems that no one knows how fox corals got their name, but they are nevertheless an attractive and moderately hardy coral. They have a unique skeleton that is very

Fox corals have a thinly folding expanding body without tentacles and a wavy lightweight skeleton similar to that of a hammer or frogspawn coral.

is a reference to the shape of the skeleton of the most common hammer corals, which is a long and thin meandering structure. Other less common hammer corals, however, may have branching skeletons.

Hammer corals have large fleshy bodies that are usually green, gray, brown or occasionally bluish in color. They are also covered by long slender tentacles with light-colored tips that when fully expanded can extend several inches from their skeleton. They will thrive under moderate to intense lighting and prefer a low to moderate current over their tentacles. Hammer corals also have long sweeper tentacles that are very powerful and can reach out several inches. Therefore they should be given anywhere from 3 to 6 inches of space beyond the maximum reach of their normal tentacles when fully expanded. The distance needed between a hammer

thin and sheetlike and is very lightweight. Fox corals will expand well beyond their skeletons, with their flesh forming large overlapping folds that are pale green in color, but they do not have any tentacles to speak of. They are not aggressive at all and are more likely to be a victim of aggression if placed too close to other species of coral. They actually seem to prefer low to moderate lighting and also prefer a very low current and usually will not fully expand under higher current conditions.

is sometimes called anchor coral has tentacle tips that are more rounded and look more like little anchors. When the name wall coral is used it

Hammer/Anchor/Wall Corals, *Euphyllia ancora* and others

The species of the group that are commonly called hammer corals are so named for the hammer-like "T" found at the end of each individual tentacle while the species that

A pair of small hammer corals that are only partially expanded. The hammer coral can expand several inches from its skeleton and use its long sweeper tentacles to damage or kill neighboring corals, so they have to be provided with plenty of room around them.

A somewhat uncommon example of a hammer coral with a thin branching skeleton.

While all of the corals in the genus *Euphyllia* have powerful stings, different hammer corals and frogspawn corals do not sting each other and can be placed in the aquarium so that they make direct contact with one another. Both hammer and frogspawn corals, however, will sting torch corals.

Below: A hammer coral and a frogspawn coral in direct contact with each other.

coral and other types of corals will of course depend on the size of the individual.

Unfortunately, hammer corals do not tolerate collection and shipping very well and typically suffer from recession from their skeletons and/or tissue necrosis. Larger pieces are more prone to such damage, because they are usually broken off larger colonies when collected. This leaves an open tear in their flesh, making them very susceptible to problems. Smaller individuals are typically found and collected whole and therefore will usually have a greater chance of survival. If a hammer coral does survive shipping, many times any area that has been damaged will heal relatively quickly and the coral will do well in the aquarium, but it is still a good idea to refrain from purchasing any coral that shows signs of tissue damage.

Frogspawn/Grape/Octopus Coral, *Euphyllia divisa*

Frogspawns are so called because their bunches of

translucent tentacles look like clumps of fertilized frogs' eggs. The tentacles also bear a resemblance to small clusters of grapes and to the sucker-covered tentacles of an octopus, hence the other common names. Like their close relative the hammer coral, they have large fleshy bodies that also extend up to several inches from their skeleton and are similar in color. Frogspawn corals will

Frogspawn coral, clearly showing the resemblance of the coral's numerous tentacles to clumps of frogs' eggs.

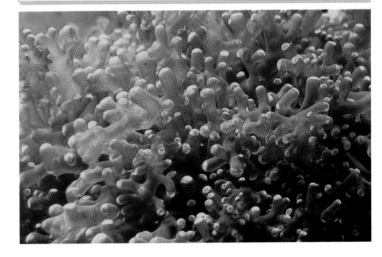

fully expand and will do well under moderate to intense lighting and a low to moderate current. They also have long sweeper tentacles that can reach out several inches and should be given anywhere from 3 to 6 inches of space beyond the maximum reach of their normal tentacles. Again, the distance needed between corals will of course depend on the size of the individuals. Frogspawn corals are collected the same way that hammer corals are and therefore also don't tolerate shipping very well. Just remember that larger individuals commonly suffer from tissue recession and/or necrosis, while smaller individuals will usually have a greater chance of survival.

Torch Coral, *Euphyllia glabrescens*

Torch corals, which have a branching skeleton topped with circular or ovoid polyps with long slender tentacles, look like fiery little torches. While torch corals are similar in color to other members of the genus *Euphyllia*, they lack any specialized tentacle tips and are easily identifiable. Torch corals fare well under moderate to intense lighting and also prefer a low to moderate current, and while they do not have especially long sweeper tentacles like their cousins, they can still reach out and sting other corals up to a few inches away and therefore should still be given at least 2 or 3 inches of space.

Torch corals also don't tolerate shipping very well and may suffer from partial tissue recession and/or necrosis. However, because

A torch coral with its long, slender tentacles waving at the ends of its multiple branches.

individual polyps are only connected by skeleton, not flesh, this condition commonly leads to the death of only one or two of the individual polyps. If this happens and one or two polyps of a large specimen die, the skeleton can be carefully broken to remove the "dead branches," leaving the rest of the colony unharmed.

FAMILY TRACHYPHYLLIIDAE
Green Open Brain Coral, *Trachyphyllia geoffroyi*

This is definitely one of the most popular and common hard corals available and is commonly placed in the same group with many other corals known as open brains. This name comes from the coral's resemblance, when fully expanded, to a small colorful

A fully expanded green open brain coral that has quite a bit of reddish color to it. The characteristic figure-8 shape of this species can be seen even when the coral is expanded.

brain; they are usually iridescent green with streaks or patches of red or brown. Green brain corals are very large individual polyps with cone-shaped skeletons that usually start as ovals and then take on a figure-eight shape as the corals grow. Green brain corals do well under moderate to intense lighting but will tolerate low light conditions. They also do well with a light to moderate current, and they tend to be very hardy. Their fleshy bodies expand well beyond their skeletons; they have very small tentacles that typically are extended at night or when being fed, but they have no sweeper tentacles and can be placed very near other corals without much risk of trouble.

The figure-8 shape of the open green brain coral is the most commonly seen form of this species.

A rare green open brain coral that looks almost as if two individual corals had been smashed together.

Red Open Brain Coral,
Trachyphyllia geoffroyi

Red brain corals are another very popular stony coral, but they tend to be harder to come by and are a little more expensive than green brain corals. They are actually the same species as the green brain coral but are simply a dark red color with some green, instead of the other way around. Also, like the green brain corals they are very large individual polyps and have the same cone-shaped skeleton that usually starts as an oval and then takes on a figure-eight shape as the coral grows. Red brain corals do well under moderate to intense lighting but also will tolerate low light conditions and will do well with a light to moderate current. They also have no sweeper tentacles and can be placed very near other corals.

A typical red open brain coral. This specimen has a bit of green in its outer body.

A beautiful example of an expanded red open brain coral. This specimen has an entirely red outer body with a bright green inner area. Specimens like it can be much more expensive than other red or green open brain corals.

FAMILY MUSSIDAE
Tooth/Flat Brain/Lobo Brain Corals, *Lobophyllia* spp.

Tooth corals are named for the large tooth-like projections and ridges on their skeletons that can often be seen through the fleshy body. Tooth corals are also considered to be open brain corals, but they come in several shapes, sizes and colors. They are most commonly green, brown or red, but may also be purple, pink or other colors as well. Tooth corals can take on a shape very similar to that of the red and green brains, but

An example of a tooth coral having a branching skeleton.

This tooth coral exhibits a highly meandering skeleton.

they can also take on a branching shape that gives rise to several individual polyps. All will do well under moderate to intense lighting and can tolerate low light conditions. They also do well with a light to moderate current, and all tend to be very hardy. They have very short feeding tentacles that are extended at night, but none have sweeper tentacles, so they can be placed very near other corals without much risk of trouble.

Tooth corals come in a variety of colors and shapes; this one has a mild pinkish cast.

Tooth/Button/Doughnut Corals,
***Scolymia* spp. and *Cynarina* spp.**

The name tooth coral is also commonly used for the members of these two genera that have skeletal features similar to those of *Lobophyllia*. These corals, however, do not have much of a variety of skeletal shapes. They are all relatively round (hence their other names, button and doughnut) and the two can be very difficult to tell apart. Many *Cynarina* have swollen translucent bodies that look very fragile, while most *Scolymia* have much thicker and tougher-looking flesh, but there are other species that fall in between. They also come in a variety of colors from deep red to brown and green. All tooth

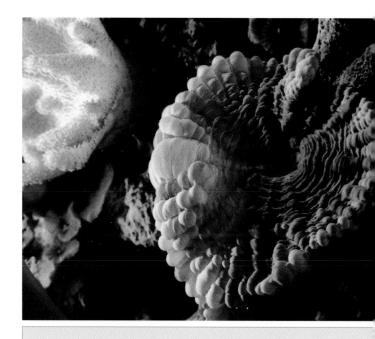

A tooth coral of the genus *Cynarina* exhibiting bulbous vesicles somewhat similar to those of the bubble corals.

Because of their rounded shape, the tooth corals of the genera *Scolymia* and *Cynarina* also are popularly known as doughnut corals and button corals. The "tooth" name, however, is much less readily apparent.

corals do well under moderate to intense lighting but will also tolerate low light conditions. They will do best with a light to moderate current, and they all tend to be very hardy. They also lack sweeper tentacles and can be placed very near other corals.

A tooth coral formed into a mound-like shape.

to intense lighting with a moderate current and also tend to be moderately hardy. Like many other corals, moon corals at first glance look as if they would not have sweeper tentacles. However, they do in fact have long, very slender sweepers that typically come out at night and can stretch a few inches to give an unwanted neighbor a relatively powerful sting. Therefore they should be given at least 2 to 3 inches of space.

FAMILY FAVIIDAE
Moon/Moonstone Corals, *Favites* spp. and *Favia* spp.

The moon, or moonstone, corals are commonly called closed brain corals because unlike open brain corals they are not overly fleshy and they typically form compact rounded skeletons looking even more like an actual brain. Moon corals in particular take on the look of the cratered surface of the moon, and while they can form encrusting colonies they more commonly form large round structures sometimes up to 5 or 6 feet in diameter. They do well under moderate

All of the photos on this page show varieties of moon corals. There is a great variance in the skeletal form, polyp shape and color exhibited by these corals. Usually the colonies that have rounded polyps belong to the genus *Favia* and those having polyps with more angular boundaries to the genus *Favites*—but there are some intermediate forms that can be much more difficult to tell apart.

Star boulder corals like this *Montastrea cavernosa* are often confused with moon corals, but they can be identified by the ring of raised ridges protruding around the edges of each polyp. Photo by Rafael Mesa.

Star Boulder Corals, *Montastrea* spp.

The star corals are another type of closed brain coral that are very similar to the moon coral, and their name comes from the ring of tiny skeletal ridges that encircle each polyp, giving the appearance of little starbursts. The "boulder" part of the name simply applies to the overall shape and color of the coral, which can look much like a fist-sized rock. They also do well under moderate to intense lighting and do best with a moderate current. They tend to be moderately hardy and, like the moon corals, they have long slender sweepers that typically come out at night and can stretch a few inches. Therefore they should also be given at least 2 to 3 inches of space.

Closeup of the surface of *Montastrea cavernosa* being traversed by a goby. The raised ridges of star boulder corals are on display here. Photo by Rafael Mesa.

48

Worm Brain Corals,
Platygyra **spp. and** *Leptoria* **spp.**

The worm brain corals are yet another variety of closed brain coral that get their name from the random meandering pattern the polyps form over their surfaces. These corals can also form large round colonies that reach sizes of over 3 feet in diameter and really look like a big green and brown or white human brain! They do well under moderate to intense lighting and prefer a moderate current. They tend to be moderately hardy; like other closed brain corals, some may have long slender sweepers.

Closeup of *Platygyra pini*, one of the numerous corals known to mini-reef fanciers as worm brain corals. Photo by Walt Deas.

A worm brain coral. The convolutions of the surface make the resemblance to the popular image of a brain unmistakable.

Above and Below: Both of these corals are individuals of the species *Blastomussa wellsi*, and while they are obviously different in color they still have very similar skeletons and polyps. The colony above was grown from a single polyp that had been broken away from a larger colony and affixed to a piece of live rock.

Blastomussa/Red Moon Coral, *Blastomussa wellsi*

Species of the genus *Blastomussa* can be found in a variety of colors, but only the red variety has a common name (red moon). The others are simply called blastomussas and usually have red or brown polyps with bright fluorescent green centers. Blastomussa coral does best under moderate lighting but will fare well under higher or lower lighting conditions. They prefer low to moderate currents and are usually very hardy. They do not have sweeper tentacles and are not aggressive toward other corals.

Trumpet/Candy/Candy Cane Corals, *Caulastrea* spp.

Trumpet corals have thinly branching skeletons that look like clumps of small horns. With colorful polyps that come in various shades of brown, green or blue on the end, the trumpet corals also look much like bundles of candies. These hardy little corals do well under moderate to intense lighting and prefer low to moderate currents. They have short sweeper tentacles but usually are not aggressive towards other nearby corals. If you are shopping for a trumpet coral, remember that any branches of the skeleton that bear injured or dead polyps can easily be broken away to salvage the remainder of the colony.

A light-colored trumpet coral. Trumpet corals come in a variety of other colors, many of which are much darker than that of this colony.

FAMILY OCULINIDAE
Galaxy/Star/Crystal Corals, *Galaxea* spp.

Galaxy corals have hundreds of short, dark-colored, closely spaced tentacles that have light-colored tips, making them look like a little galaxy of stars. They require moderate to intense lighting but do well in a wide range of currents. Unfortunately, they are not particularly hardy and even under good conditions will sometimes slowly succumb to tissue recession. Galaxy corals also have very long sweeper tentacles that carry a powerful sting and are sometimes 4 or 5 inches in length. Because they are aggressive and are not hardy, they are not recommended for beginners.

A galaxy coral with its normal tentacles extended. Not seen here are the numerous thin sweeper tentacles that can quickly dispatch nearby other corals.

FAMILY FUNGIIDAE
Short-Tentacle Plate/Disk Corals,
Fungia **spp. and** *Cycloseris* **spp.**

Short-tentacle plate corals are so called because of the relatively flat circular shape of their skeletons and the very short tentacles that cover their bodies. Each individual plate coral is actually one very large polyp with a large centrally located mouth. Plate corals do well under most any lighting conditions and are not too picky about current either as long as it doesn't blow them away. They are very hardy and do not possess sweeper tentacles, but they still should not be allowed to touch any other types of coral. Their only particular requirement is that they be placed flat on the bottom of the aquarium.

This small short-tentacle plate coral started out as a tiny bud at the tip of a piece of live rock. Over a period of about six months the bud grew into a coral the size of a half dollar.

A not-so-common short-tentacle plate coral. This variety is commonly called a purple disk coral.

A long-tentacle plate coral with its tentacles extended.

When placed on the bottom of an aquarium, long-tentacle plate corals like this are frequently mistaken for anemones.

Long-Tentacle Plate/Disk Corals, *Heliofungia* spp.

Obviously, long-tentacle plate corals have tentacles that are longer than those of the short-tentacle plate corals. In fact, these tentacles can reach lengths of over 6 inches. Long-tentacle plate corals also do well under most any lighting conditions and are not too picky about current either. They are very hardy and while they do not possess sweeper tentacles, the normal tentacles are long enough to reach out and sting other corals up to several inches away. So, like the short-tentacle plate corals, they also should be placed flat on the bottom of the aquarium, but they will need to be given a bit of room to stretch out.

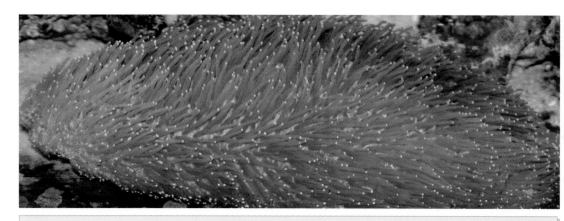

A slipper coral. The only easy-to-spot distinction between the slipper corals and the tongue corals is the groove that runs down the middle of the tongue coral's skeleton, making it look a little more tongue-like. The slipper corals have no such groove.

Tongue/Slipper Corals, *Herpolitha limax* and *Polyphyllia* spp.

Tongue corals look just like a big hairy tongue, and slipper corals have similar features that look something like a fuzzy house slipper, making it very easy to see how both got their names. Like the plate corals, tongue and slipper corals do well under most any lighting conditions and currents. They are also very hardy and lack sweeper tentacles; they should always be placed flat on the bottom of the aquarium.

FAMILY PORITIDAE
Flowerpot/Ball Corals, *Goniopora* spp.

Flowerpot corals when fully extended look like a beautiful bouquet of brown, green or bluish flowers. However, their impressive appearance does not make up for their pitiful survival rate. The elongated polyps of flowerpot corals will expand fully under moderate to intense lighting with a moderate current, but with rare exception they simply do not last long-term in aquariums. They also commonly do not ship well,

ABOVE
A flowerpot coral with its tentacles extended.

BELOW
A flowerpot coral with its tentacles fully retracted. Not much to look at!

Closeup of a *Herpolitha* (not *H. limax*) coral showing the groove running through the skeleton. Photo by Dr. Leon P. Zann.

suffering from tissue recession, tissue loss and death, and while they are tempting they should be avoided. If you still choose to try a flowerpot coral, keep in mind that while they lack sweeper tentacles, their polyps can be very long and will damage other corals. So make sure to leave enough room around a flowerpot coral that it does not touch other corals when it is fully expanded.

Jewel Corals, *Porites* spp.

The corals of the genus *Porites* come in a wide variety of shapes and colors, the skeleton taking on a branching, massive or encrusting form with colors ranging from green, brown or blue to pink or purple. They are named for the tiny "jewels" that can be seen at

A jewel coral covered by tightly spaced polyps with numerous small tentacles. Jewel corals are available in a wide variety of shapes, colors and sizes.

A jewel coral "rind" that was purchased on a small piece of live rock. This small patch of coral has the potential to grow into a beautiful branching colony within a couple of years.

the center of each polyp. It is common to find small spots of jewel coral on live rock that will often grow into large colonies under good conditions. Jewel corals also require intense lighting and a moderate to strong current; they are not aggressive toward other corals. They typically do not ship well, but many are moderately hardy in the aquarium.

FAMILY DENDROPHYLLIIDAE
Turban/Pagoda/Cup Corals, *Turbinaria* spp.

Members of this genus also come in a variety of shapes. Some are named for their curved turbinate skeletons, while other types look exactly like a pagoda or a large flattened cup. All do best under moderate to intense lighting with a moderate current. None have sweeper

A common form of turban coral; this one looks like a birdbath or large ceremonial cup. Other forms vary greatly in shape, but all are wrapped by a thin layer of flesh covered by many large polyps.

tentacles and none are aggressive toward other corals. Most are at least moderately hardy, and many are very hardy.

Yellow Scroll Coral, *Turbinaria reniformis*

Scroll coral can look similar to turban coral but is usually thinner, looking just like an unrolled scroll of paper with more open curves. Yellow scroll coral does best under moderate to intense lighting and prefers a moderate current. Like other *Turbinaria* they do not have sweeper tentacles and are not aggressive toward other corals. However, while most *Turbinaria* are very hardy, the scroll corals are typically more fickle and may suffer from tissue recession even under good conditions.

Sun/Sunflower Coral, *Tubastrea faulkneri*

Sun corals, which are named for their bright orange

A colony of sun coral with polyps retracted.

color and the sunburst appearance of their expanded polyps, are very unusual. Unlike almost all other corals available to the hobbyist, sun corals do not have zooxanthellae and do not need strong lighting to thrive. The downside of this condition is that for sun corals to thrive

A large specimen of yellow scroll coral. Like the turban coral, this coral's skeleton is covered by a thin layer of tissue, but the polyps are much more widely spaced and are much smaller.

This sun coral colony's polyps are partially extended in an effort to capture food particles.

Above and Below: Two varieties of the richly varietal genus *Acropora*, which contains corals that differ widely in colors and shapes and branch thicknesses.

they must be regularly fed tiny bits of meat or brine shrimp using an eyedropper. If you are not ready to give this kind of attention to a coral, then stay clear of the sun coral. If you wish to try one, keep in mind that they can be placed in any part of the aquarium, even under a rock ledge with very low light levels. And contrary to the belief of some, they are not adversely affected by intense

lighting as long as they are given time to slowly acclimate to it. They prefer a low to moderate current and are not aggressive, but remember that without good care they will not last long in an aquarium.

FAMILY ACROPORIDAE
Acropora/Staghorn/Table Corals,
***Acropora* spp.**
Acropora is a large genus of corals that has well over 300 individual species, many of which are very difficult to tell apart. A few are named for the overall shape of the skeleton (staghorn looks like deer antlers, etc.), but most are named after their individual color (purple acropora, yellow acropora, etc.). This can lead to some confusion when it comes to telling species apart, because each species can come in several colors.

Taken from above the aquarium, this photo of an acropora clearly shows that each of the branches is tipped by a relatively large individual polyp. Such polyps are called terminal polyps, and their presence is a good identification guide helping to separate acroporas from other small-tentacled corals.

Acropora is a very fast-growing coral and is popular with many hobbyists because it can be fragmented to create dozens of individuals. This is done by breaking up a large specimen and gluing the pieces to various pieces of live rock throughout the aquarium. Under good conditions each little fragment will eventually grow into a separate colony. Acroporas will thrive under intense lighting but will also live under moderate lighting; they prefer a strong current.

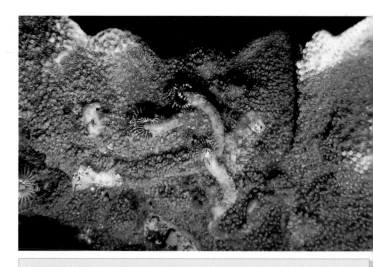

A *Montipora* species with embedded worms. Photo by Walt Deas.

A typical staghorn-shaped acropora.

Acroporas commonly do not handle shipping very well. Many colonies will arrive dead, but if they make it for a few days they tend to be moderately to very hardy. Acroporas do not have sweeper tentacles but will use acontia against other corals they comes into contact with, so avoid letting them touch other corals.

Velvet Corals, *Montipora sp.*
   Like jewel corals, members of this genus of coral come in a very wide variety of shapes and colors from red to yellow to blue, all of which have a fuzzy velvet appearance. Also like jewel corals, small spots of velvet coral are commonly seen on high-quality live rock and will often grow into massive colonies relatively quickly. They require intense lighting and a moderate to strong current; they are not aggressive toward other corals. They typically do not ship well, but many are moderately to very hardy in the aquarium.

FAMILY POCILLOPORIDAE
Bird's Nest Coral, *Seriatopora hystrix*
   Bird's nest coral resembles the staghorns but has a very thin, finely branching skeleton. These corals require

Bird's nest coral gets its popular name from its supposed resemblance to a bunch of small twigs like those used by some birds to build nests. Usually each branch is very thin and ends in a point and is covered by exceptionally small polyps that form tiny parallel rows. Photo by Walt Deas.

intense lighting and a moderate to strong current to do well. They also lack sweeper tentacles, but as with acropora should not be allowed to touch other corals. Unfortunately this coral typically does not ship well, and even if it survives in the home aquarium tends to not be very hardy.

Cauliflower Corals, *Pocillopora* spp.

Cauliflower corals look something like a colorful head of cauliflower and closely resemble acropora, but they tend to have much larger polyps. They fare well in moderate to intense lighting and also need a strong current. Again, these corals typically do not ship well, but under good conditions they tend to be fairly hardy in the aquarium. They also lack sweeper tentacles but still should not be allowed to touch other corals.

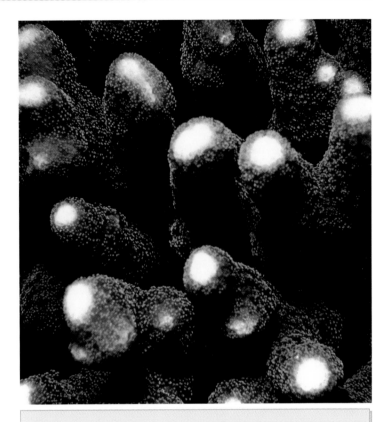

Closeup of a cauliflower coral, showing the tips of the branches. Photo by Walt Deas.

Cauliflower coral looks similar to the acroporas, but it lacks the terminal polyp at the tip of each skeletal branch. Instead, the ends of the branches are covered by numerous polyps. Photo by Walt Deas.

Cat's Paw Coral, *Stylophora pistillata*

This coral also resembles acropora but has thick, heavy branches that look like fuzzy cats' paws. They require intense lighting and a strong current, and while they lack sweeper tentacles they should not be allowed to touch other corals. Cat's paw corals also typically do not ship well, and even under good conditions tend to not fare well in the aquarium.

FAMILY MERULINIDAE
Ridge Coral, *Merulina* spp.

Ridge corals are named for the tiny ridges that run over the entire skeleton. Ridge corals are very demanding and require intense lighting

Cat's paw coral is covered by small polyps that give it a fuzzy texture. This texture, in combination with the thick rounded branches of the skeleton, gives the coral its name. Photo by Walt Deas.

This ridge coral has a form dominated by short knobby projections. Many other ridge corals have much flatter skeletons and look like pieces of wavy corduroy.

and a strong current. They are not aggressive toward other corals, but they may not ship well, are typically not very hardy and are not commonly available to hobbyists.

Horn/Branch Corals, *Hydnophora* spp.

Horn corals are usually a beautiful green color and may look very desirable, but be warned: looks are deceiving. While during daytime there are no obvious tentacles, at night horn corals can quickly dispatch nearby corals with exceptionally long sweeper tentacles. These sweepers can reach out several inches, so you will have to make sure to give this coral plenty of room.

Hydnophora rigida, a horn coral and therefore one of the most aggressive available to aquarists. While it is apparently free of tentacles, at night exceptionally long sweeper tentacles can reach out and deliver a deadly sting to nearby corals. This coral *must* be given plenty of room. Photo by Walt Deas.

Horn corals typically require intense lighting and a strong current to thrive, but are not particularly hardy even when provided with those conditions. Because of this, and their aggressiveness towards other corals, they are not recommended for beginning hobbyists.

Hydnophora exesa, another species of horn coral. Photo by Walt Deas.

A cactus coral. This species is *Pavona decussata.* Photo by Walt Deas.

FAMILY AGARICIIDAE
Cactus Corals, *Pavona* spp.

These corals can look just like a clump of prickly little cacti. They come in leafy and frilly varieties. They require moderate to intense lighting and a moderate to strong current. They are usually moderately hardy in the aquarium and lack sweeper tentacles, but they still should not be allowed to touch other corals.

Cactus corals have a wide range of skeletal forms, from compact to open and leafy. Many have a rough-looking, almost prickly texture, which is what gives this group its common name. Photo by Walt Deas.

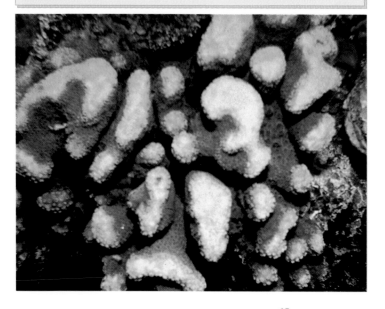

Elephant Skin Coral, *Pachyseris rugosa*

Elephant skin coral looks exactly like what it is called. It is darkly colored and has a rough crinkled surface like that of an elephant. Elephant

Elephant skin coral, *Pachyseris rugosa*. This piece has been epoxied to a rock in an upright position but actually prefers a horizontal position so that more of its surface is directly exposed to light.

skin corals thrive under intense lighting but will tolerate moderate lighting. They also do best with a moderate to strong current. Elephant skin corals lack sweeper tentacles and tend to be moderately to very hardy.

Millepora tenella, a dangerous fire coral. Photo by Walt Deas.

A nice specimen of lettuce coral. This particular colony has a form dominated by a number of tightly spaced spikes, but others may have a more open and leafy form.

Hydrozoa, and *Millepora* is the only genus in the order that produces a hard skeleton. A fire coral's anatomy is somewhat different from that of the stony corals, but to the hobbyist the skeleton looks basically the same as that of many of the small-polyped stony corals. Fire corals have earned their name   from the very painful sting they can deliver if touched; the sting can burn the flesh even through a diver's wetsuit.

FAMILY PECTINIIDAE
Lettuce Corals, *Pectinia* spp .

These corals have a frilly skeleton that often looks something like a small colored head of lettuce. They require moderate to intense lighting and a moderate to strong current. They are not aggressive, but they also are not hardy at all and rarely survive shipping. For this reason lettuce corals are not commonly seen for sale.

CLASS HYDROZOA
Order Milleporina

FAMILY MILLEPORIDAE
Fire Corals, *Millepora* spp.

In mentioning the fire corals we've left the class Anthozoa, because fire corals are members of the order Milleporina in the class

Millepora alficornis, a fire coral, shown here covering a gorgonian and with the sponge *Clathria calla*. Photo by Rafael Mesa.

Needless to say, they should be handled with great care! If they are handled when the stinging polyps are retracted they can be *carefully* placed into the aquarium. Fire corals thrive under moderate to intense lighting and prefer strong current. They tend to be very hardy, and despite their sting they have no sweeper tentacles and thus can be placed relatively near other corals as long as they do not make contact.

CLASS ANTHOZOA
Order Stolonifera

FAMILY CLAVULARIIDAE
Organ-Pipe Corals, *Tubipora* spp.

Here we're back into the class Anthozoa again, but in a different subclass (Octocorallia, also called Alcyonaria) from that of the stony, or hard, corals. The latter are in the subclass Hexacorallia, also referred to as Zoantharia. Members of the order Stolonifera are another "false" coral commonly seen in reef aquariums. Organ-pipe corals are named after the intricate skeleton they produce, which is made of tiny straw-like tubes that are loosely bound together like the pipes of a church organ. The skeleton of organ-pipe corals is also unique because of its dark red color; it is often used to decorate fish-only marine aquariums. Organ-pipe corals do well under moderate to intense lighting but will tolerate low light conditions. They also do well with a light to strong current, and they tend to be moderately hardy. They have no sweeper tentacles and thus can be placed near other corals.

Above: Organ-pipe coral is popular for the reef aquarium and typically does well under a variety of conditions. This closeup of the bright polyps of an organ-pipe coral shows that each polyp has a ring of eight tentacles, marking it as an octocorallid, not a hexacorallid. Polyps of the true stony corals usually come in multiples of twelve.

Below: The red color and the arrangement of thin tubes produced by each polyp are characteristic of the organ-pipe corals.